The Creation of a Gem - You!

The Creation of a Gem -
You!

Penny Dale

authorHOUSE®

AuthorHouse™
1663 Liberty Drive
Bloomington, IN 47403
www.authorhouse.com
Phone: 1-800-839-8640

First published by AuthorHouse   07/27/2011

ISBN: 978-1-4634-3447-2 (sc)
ISBN: 978-1-4634-3446-5 (ebk)

Library of Congress Control Number: 2011912145

Printed in the United States of America

Any people depicted in stock imagery provided by Thinkstock are models, and such images are being used for illustrative purposes only.
Certain stock imagery © Thinkstock.

This book is printed on acid-free paper.

CONTENTS

INTRODUCTION

I CAN REMEMBER when my sister and I wanted to spend sister time, we would get a blanket from my dad's wash room and lay it on the grass near mom's Ash tree in the front yard. We would look as far as our eyes could see, if by chance, we could see God's Heaven.

I imagine there are a lot of people beside myself that tried to visual in their mind the beauty of Heaven. It is by no means compatible to this earth. Don't get me wrong. Our earth has some awesome and incredible places to visit if sightseeing or traveling is your game.

In 2 Peter 3:7 and 10 says one day heaven and earth will pass away with a great noise and the elements that help to create what we see will melt with fervent heat.

When all things are accomplished, there will be a new heaven and earth. "A New Beginning" As I was studying about this new heaven and earth, my mind stopped me on the verse that talks on the foundation of the wall of the New Jerusalem.

Do you have a favorite color? Most people, I have found, have more than one favorite color. The foundation of the wall has twelve different colors. And just maybe your favorite color is one of them.

REVELATION 21:19 AND 20

"And the foundation of the wall of the city were garnished with all manner of precious stones. The first foundation was Jasper; the second, sapphire; the third, a chalcedony; the fourth, an emerald; the fifth, sardonyx; the sixth, sardius; the seventh, chrysolite; the eight, beryl; the ninth, a topaz; the tenth, a chrysoprasus; the eleventh, a jacinth; the twelfth, an amethyst".

To sum it up, what "fineness".For those of you that are fascinated by stones, has the thought of how the stones were birth ever crossed your mind? And, of all the gems in the world, why did God choose the twelve stones he chose to be a part of the wall of the New Jerusalem?

Come with me, venture out and discover what makes these stones so special.

CHAPTER ONE

JASPER IS THE first foundation. Let me give you some history about this stone. This stone comes in assortment of color, patterns and bands. If one looks closely, the patterns resemble landscapes, mountains and valleys. When I read this, my mind immediately thought of "Trails".

The quartz contains twenty percent of foreign material and the result is it is rarely uniform in color. Therefore, it may be multicolored, striped and possible spotted.

It is interesting how this stone, Jasper and Jacob, Isaac son, have in common. It is one of the oldest stories in the Bible about two brothers, which happens to be twins and where the oldest twin serves the youngest.

Unfortunately, sometimes in families, there are issues where some of the family members just can't get along. This family so happens to be one of those.

One day, Esau came in from the field hungry. He saw Jacob cooking some pottage and he asked Jacob if he could have some of his pottage because he felt faint.

In return, Jacob asked Esau to sell to him his birthright. At this point, his birthright was meaningless to him because he felt like he was about to die. He sold his birthright for food.

As time went on, Isaac felt death approaching. He called his oldest son, Esau to see him. When he came in to see his dad, Isaac told him that he was dying and he wanted to bless him and made a request wanting some venison.

All this time, Rebekah heard their conversation. She quickly went to Jacob and told him what happened between his dad and brother. She devised a very clever hideous plan to where Jacob would get Isaac's blessing instead of Esau.

She told Jacob to get the meat and she would fix it the way his dad likes it. When he brought back the meat, she cooked it and gave it to Jacob to give to his dad. Before presenting the meat, Rebekah took Esau's raiment and laid it upon Jacob and then she took the skin of goats and laid them on Jacob's hand and neck for a precaution if Isaac wanted to touch Jacob's flesh.

Her plan worked. Isaac blessed Jacob. When Esau came in from hunting, he prepared the meat like always and went into his father's house to feed him. He called for his dad to come and eat. When Isaac came to the dinner table, he wanted to know who was there with him earlier if it was not Esau. For whomever it was will be truly be blessed. Jacob got the family's blessing.

In turn, this made Esau furious. He planned to slay Jacob after his dad's death. The news of Esau's plan reached Rebekah. She came up with a plan that would save both her son's lives.

She wanted Jacob to have a wife but not any of the women of Canaan. She went to Isaac and told him how she felt about the women and she used their way of living to help lure Isaac's decision in agreement to hers; which was to send him to her brother in Padam-aram. Again, her plan worked. So, Isaac sent Jacob to Padam-aram where Rebekah's brother lives to find a wife.

From here, the story really gets interesting. Jacob heads off on his first frontier "not knowing" the encounters that awaits him. He finally gets to the area where Rebekah's brother lives. He meets the family he never knew. Jacob stays one month and Laban went to Jacob to ask him what he would charge in wages to work for him.

Jacob told Laban that he loves his daughter Rachel and he will serve him seven years for her hand in marriage. Laban agreed with Jacob terms and the seven years of time for Jacob seemed to go by quickly.

As the seventh year drew closer, he anticipated the day of accomplishment to finalize the agreement to have Rachel as his wife. So, he thought. As it turned out, the custom of those days, the oldest goes first in marriage before the youngest.

In order to receive Rachel in marriage, he had to fulfill one week with Leah, the oldest daughter, and serve yet another seven years to Laban. Jacob loves Rachel so much that he agreed to Laban terms.

As time proceeded, children were born. When the eleventh child was born, Jacob went to Laban and asked him for his wives and children for it was time to go back to Canaan.

Laban quickly responded back and asked Jacob to tarry; for, he has been blessed while he has been with him. Jacob agreed to stay but there was a catch. Laban asked him what would be his price. Jacob's response, "Thou shalt not give me anything: if thou wilt do this thing for me, I will again feed and keep thy flock". Jacob told him that he would remove all the speckled and spotted cattle and goats and all the brown sheep. This would be his when the time came to go back to Canaan. Laban agreed.

That day, Laban went thru the entire herd and removed the ringstraked and spotted male goats and the speckled and spotted female goats. If there were any white, he took those and all the brown among the sheep. These, he gave to his sons. They separated themselves a three-day journey.

Jacob came up with a brilliant plan that would be to his advantage. He gathered three kinds of tree bark. Poplar, Almond and Plane. Then, he took each one and stripped off pieces of the bark, exposing the white inside and laid them in the gutters in the water troughs; so when, the cattle came to drink, they would mate in the presence of the rods.

When doing so, the flocks brought forth stripped, speckled and spotted offspring. My question is why he chose those three trees. I was curious; so, I began to study each tree's trait. I discovered that each tree has uniqueness about them.

PopLAR TREE

Has a smooth, nearly white bark that roughens and darkens with age. The bark is recognized by its anti-inflammatory and pain relieving properties. Also, it is used to treat those who suffer Arthritis and Rheumatic aches and pain.

When someone is sick in the family, Poplar is used to lower the fever especially for those who suffer from Rheumatoid Arthritis.

As a stimulant, the bark acts as a tonic remedy in the treatment of patients suffering from Anorexia. It has antiseptic qualities and acts as an astringent in treating for U.T.I. and the Irritable Bowel Syndrome.

Planted to clean contaminated ground water along streams, rivers and at water treatment sites. When planted along rivers and streams, the Poplar tree helps with restoration and controls erosion and to create a wildlife habitat.

AlMONd TREE

Almond means "Awakening" and promise of a new life and hope. It has been known that the Almond tree is the first to awake and rise from the hand of old winter.

The Almond is among the "best fruits" of Canaan and is filled with abundant supply of essential oil. In cooking, the Almond is a great substitute for Olive oil. Massage Therapist around the world used the oil from the Almond to lubricate the skin during massage sessions.

In health benefits, as you apply the Almond oil to the skin, the oil improves complexion and the movement of food through the colon and prevention of cancer.

People of today looks for retirement and maybe to travel to places they could not do while they worked. The Almond has a great success influencing "Longevity" so that you can do those things you want to do when the time comes.

Not long ago, there were three factors discovered about Almond. In its possession the Almond has anti-inflammatory, immunity boosting and anti-hepatotoxicity effects.

PLANE TREE

The bark from this tree throws off all impurity yearly by shedding its outer bark, leaving the shades of different colors: white, gray, green and yellow.

The tree has a resistance to disease and air pollution. Grows along watercourses where there is sufficient soil moisture to sustain it.

It is amazing to see the seminaries of each tree as well as the differences that each one holds. All three works together in a special bonding matter. Yet, each one has its own path of life and purpose to fulfill.

During our walk of life, we will encounter opportunities to accomplish our greatest desire; however, along with those desires come with a cost.

We will be able to account every struggle, difficulty, brokenness even our tears while achieving our goal. We will not be the same person in the end as we were in the beginning.

No mountain or hill will be too great. Our accomplishments, no matter how great or small, will bring us into a higher dimension with our creator. He is there all the while, either holding our hand or carrying us thru. He is our provider. Whatever we need, the provision will be met.

Perseverance leaves its mark upon us as a great conqueror. Win or lose, there are no boundaries. Seeks for those who are willing to come up to the plate and venture out of their comfort zone and leaves a legacy for others to follow.

CHAPTER TWO

AS A CHILD growing up, my parents grew lots of fruits and vegetables. When the time came to pick the garden, mom would either seal the veggies in bags or she would can them instead and put them up in the storage cabinet in the garage.

Canning took up most of her time. She would get out the old pressure cooker that was stored in the cabinet and laid out all the jars she would think she would need and the canning began.

All fruits and vegetables have a required process time when canning in the pressure cooker. The first step, mom would cook her vegetables till they were done. Then, she would pour the cooked veggies into the jars and sealed the lid. The pressure cooker only held five or six cans at a time.

When the heat began to cook the vegetables, she would watch the temperature gage carefully. She did not want to pressure cook the jars too long; for if she did, all of her work would be wasted. Cracked jars and spoiled vegetables would be the end results.

Unlike mom's harvest, regions of our earth experiences constant pressure all the time. The reason behind this pressure is the earth's tectonic plates shifting. There are twelve plates that make up the earth's outer shell.

Churning currents in the molten rock below thrusts the plates to venture out and conquer new territories. Unfortunately, people who live along the plate's line lives in a constant fear of "Not Knowing" if they are going to experience an earthquake.

Every year the plates move a few centimeters. They are constantly moving in different directions. The plates may move apart from each other, collide with one another or one plate is forced under another. In any of these events, there is change and purpose.

Change is universal. For some, it is the enemy while on the other hand it is a friend. Billions of years ago deep within the earth, below the earth's crust, in the mantle, change was introduced by high temperature and pressure. As the magma cooled down, it formed igneous rock deposits and Corundum was incorporated in those deposits. Transformation was not finished.

As the years passed by, the plate's continued to reshape our earth. As this change progressed, the igneous rocks transformed into sedimentary and metamorphic rocks as it move closer to the surface.

Corundum crystals went thru a continuous weathering and erosion stage for many years. Finally, the crystals were washed down on the slopes of mountains and deposited in rivers and streams. Here will be their home till someone discovers them.

Corundum shares its mask in three colorful rays: colorless, deep red, called Ruby and Sapphire. Sapphires are valued for their luster. Meaning, their ability to reflect light like a mirror. Their hardness ranks second place. They have a very low chance of getting scratched.

I find this amazing. The second thing that God Created and the second foundation of the wall of Jerusalem have something in common. Do you know what it is?

In Genesis 1:3-4 says, "And God said, let there be light and there was light. God saw the light that it was good and he separated the light from the darkness".

As I mentioned earlier, Corundum is birth in the mantle of the earth. Over time, the earth experienced a season of transformation. The transitions the Corundum had to endure were necessary to reach its destiny. It took several centuries of persevering to reach the earth's surface. It came out of darkness and into light.

Cutting Sapphire requires more time because of the great detail involved. They are cut on a precise angle so that the Light can reflect and refract the different angles of the stone.

If the craftsman can bring the Light out that enters and exits the stone, it will be more to the advantage of the stone; for, it is in the eye of the beholder's desire to see the stone's glory.

Daniel 3:11

There is a familiar story that comes to my mind that reflects the beginning stages of the Sapphire gem.

In the third year of King Jehoiakim, King Nebuchadnezzar of Babylon conquered Jerusalem. During his reign, he made an image of gold. The height of this image was threescore cubits and the breadth was six cubits.

King Nebuchadnezzar made a degree that when you hear the sound of the cornet, flute, harp, sackbut, psaltery and dulcimer you must fall down and worship the golden image.

One day, the musicians came to play their instruments and immediately the people bowed down and worshipped the image; except Shadrach, Meshach and Abednego. And, this infuriated the king.

He called for a meeting. He asked the three men is it true they did not bow down to his god. He warned them the next time when the musicians came to play, to bow down and if they did not, they would be put into the fiery furnace. The musicians came again and played their instruments. Again, the men refused to bow down. It was ordered to throw them into the furnace.

It was so hot that the attendants who put the three men inside the furnace died. Shadrach, Meshach and Abednego fell down bound in the fire. A little while after, Nebuchadnezzar looked inside the furnace and was astonished. He inquired the council did they not throw in three men. They replied back, yes.

He told the council there were not three men but four and not bound but walking in the mist of the fire and the fourth man looked like the Son of God.

Even in the furnace of affliction, we are not alone for Jesus is with us. When the people of this world put us into the fiery furnace, whether it is because we dress, act or speak differently, God uses the fire to bring out our impurities. As a result, since we are different, the Refiner's fire leaves his rainbow of colors within us.

CHAPTER THREE

NEWSPAPER, MAGAZINES, TELEVISION and radio programs occupy our society. They have a strong influence on the people's heart and mind by slowly injecting information on what is happening in their local area and places in other countries whether it may be good or bad.

One way to avoid the news is too stay away from it; however, there are some that thrives on what is happening around them. For myself, watching our local weather can depress me; especially if, I hear it will be raining with a strong SE wind on a day I have a race. Just hearing that can bring on discouragement and thoughts of not finishing.

This brings us to the third stone, Chalcedony. This stone is extremely porous. Porous means absorptive, full of holes or space, like in the skin or soil. Since the stone has this ability, it takes dye easily and is frequently enhanced. If you decide to own this type of stone, you may want to protect your investment from harsh chemicals and extreme temperature.

As I study this stone, a song comes to mind. In children's church before the director would teach, they would sing songs. One in particular comes to mind, "Oh Be Careful". The writer expresses four physical properties to be careful. The intent of the song is to prepare the younger generation to watch and stay alert so they won't be tempted.

A similar warning Jesus gave his disciples while they were in the garden on the night he was betrayed. In Matthew 26:41, Jesus asked the disciples to watch and pray so that they would not enter into temptation.

Temptation approached Eve in Eden. The serpent drew her a vivid picture in her mind what "Life" would be like if she took of the fruit from the Tree of Good and Evil.

She welcomed the words of an imaginary sitcom authored by the serpent himself and temptation was birth.

To tempt means: to risk the danger of; to entice to do wrong by promise of pleasure or gain.

The words "you will be like God" entered into her mind and instead of exiting thru her ears, the words pursued to her heart and there the serpent had the upper hand. He introduced to her a life filled with opportunity and advancement.

The more time she pondered those words in her heart, she turned to the tree and while she glazed, her mind began to flow on how this opportunity could be used to her advantage to make her wise. For the first time, she saw the tree of Good and Evil in a different light and welcomed the invitation of want.

Don't get me wrong. To want something is great; but, it is how one achieves that desire or want is what is important. Temptation surrounds us every day in a variety of ways. All one needs to do is look around. I may not be tempted in the same way some are, but none of the less, still tempted.

This stone has an awesome attribute. But before I get into telling about this characteristic, let me ask you another question. Are you saved? If you are, you have the "Word" living inside of you. He leads and guides us thru those temptation times and provides a way of escape, so we can endure it.

Let's say you are invited by friends to go out on the town for the evening. You thought about it for a while and decided it might be good for you to get out for you have not been anywhere for a long time. Dinner went well. You ask the waiter if you could have a cup of coffee with cream. As you are waiting for that cup to arrive, you notice one of the members of the group is looking at you. You responded back with a smile. You turn your eyes immediately away and start to look for the waiter that will be bringing your coffee. As you bring back your attention to the table, the member is acting too friendly towards you.

You are stunned by their behavior; for, they are acting way out of their character. In your heart you ask the Holy Spirit for guidance. Upon your request, he turns the situation around in your favor.

The Holy Spirit is the best protector for God's children. The more we grow in God's Word, the more territory we give him to reign with us.

17

Remember earlier I said this stone has an awesome attribute? Chalcedony, among other quarts, allows chemical solutions to infiltrate inside the stone. Resulting a chemical reaction in a more durable color than just coating the surface. It has been known that these chemical solutions may either completely stain the stone or part.

There are a lot of influences in the world that will try to come upon us and separate us from Christ. He gives us the choice to either follow the world or come and dine with him. The more we spend time with him, the less of the world is in us, and believe me the world see the transformation within you and will try its best to win you back.

Keep in the "Word" thru out your day. Sing choruses while you work and read his word after you had your meal. In the book of John, chapter 15 and verse 19 says, "If ye were of the world, the world would love his own: but because ye are not of the world, but I have chosen you out of the world, therefore the world hateth you".

To put this in respective, within this stone, there are veins. The chemical solution they use to color these stones cannot penetrate thru them. If you buy Chalcedony and the stonecutter cuts the stone with a vein present, the chemical solution will stain around the vein. The more we include Christ in all areas of our lives, the less the world dominates (stains).

CHAPTER FOUR

DO YOU LIKE to travel? Answering for myself, "Oh Yea". It does not really matter if I am a passenger or the driver. I love to just get away and be lost for a few hours and let my mind rest and watch the countryside unfold its beauty.

My parents are from Anderson County in Texas and springtime is just awesome. The Dogwood trees are in season and their blooms are just breath taking. Looking from a distance, you cannot cipher where the tree is because of its blooms intertwining with the green foliage of other trees. Looking at all angles, it is just awesome.

Winter has passed and the season of New Beginning is on the horizon. A time of change from death to life of restoration.

I live in an area in my hometown known as the historic section. Every Spring as I observe, lawns get a facelift, trees are pruned and what is dead in the flower garden is pulled up and replaced with vibrant colors of fresh Daffodils, Azaleas and Cosmos.

We open up our home and welcome the flesh air and while we enjoy a cup of coffee on the porch, we can actually smell the restoration of Spring taking place.

New Beginnings, in conjunction with growing, can be frightening; while on the other hand, can be adventurous. That is what life is about. "Adventure." Every day when we wake up from our rest, it is another day for accomplishments. It does not matter how old or young we are or how well and bad we look. Our accomplishments are all well written on the staircase of life. Engraved by our Creator never to be forgotten.

Our accomplishments are part of his garden. We plant our plans into the soil hoping that the seeds of desire will prosper and live to fulfill its purpose.

As that purpose makes its finish, our Creator moves us up to the next step where he works in us to bring forth as a testament unto himself and when the stairs run out, there he will be giving us our reward for a job well done.

CHAPTER FIVE

GENESIS 1:28, "THEN God blessed them, and God said to them, be fruitful and multiply, fill the earth and subdue it . . ."

Sardonxy represents the journey of Life. Online dictionary, the editor will give you twenty-five amazing definitions all about life. As a participant, I have decided that Life is one big mystery.

Most of us have a routine. We get up and eat breakfast, get dressed and arrive at our job site at the appointed time. After completing between 8 to 12 hours of work, we get into our car and prepare ourselves what lies ahead; for some, it is "suppertime".

An hour or two after supper, we allow our body and mind to rest only to get up the next morning to do our routine all over again. To most of us, this is our way of Life. You want to know a secret? As old as I am today, working 3 days of twelve's and a half a day and still cook and clean and run errands is just amazing.

In the book of Ecclesiastes in the third chapter, Solomon wrote, "To every thing there is a season, and a time to every purpose under heaven: A time to be born, and a time to die;"

Between verses one of chapter three to verse eight, there is a season between each comma. For instance, in verse two, "A time to born, and a Time to die" between Life and Death, it is a season.

Only the Creator knows the length of each of his creation's life span. Some of us will see our great grandchildren, while others will only experience having birth their first and due to complications during labor, the Creator has called the little one home.

Teachers, counselors of high school and Sunday school teachers alike starts teaching teenagers about the journey of Life when they began their eleventh year of school; preparing and counseling them for the road that lies ahead of them.

In this journey of Life, there are so many pathways to choose from. The main thing to remember is, allow the Creator to take you on the path that he wants you to take. As long as you stay on the path he has chosen for you, he will be there with his right hand upon you.

It will not always be a smooth path to travel. There will be curves, bumps, overpasses and stop signs. The more you grow in him; you will encounter bigger obstacles to conquer.

For those who like to adventure to the left or to the right of the path the Creator has in store for you, my advice is to be careful. Look around you. If you don't see any signs of his presence, you don't need to be on this path. Backup and turn around and return to the path that the Creator has designed just for you.

CHAPTER SIX

DID YOU KNOW that all of us have a warrior's type mentality? And most people today when talking about a warrior their mind focuses on a male fighting in combat with artillery flying in space all around them. Visualize the combat zone with bombs dropping from a F1-17, tankers in route and infantry in pursuit of the enemy.

What about the warrior sitting at home watching the nightly news on CBS or the warrior sitting at his or her desk in the city's administration building on main street or the one driving to work? Does not sound like they are in war; but, they are.

"War" is not only about people in combat clothing and hiding in the bushes waiting for the enemy to arrive to exchange gunpowder. All people including "great" to the "least" is at some type of war.

In Ephesians 6:12 says, "For we wrestle not against flesh and blood but against principalities, against powers, against the ruler of darkness of this world, against spiritual wickedness in high places."

Our country's tax money provides all of the armed forces with the necessary equipment needed to protect them while in pursuit of the enemy and for home base.

Every day, I pray for my family's protection. I ask Jesus to watch and cover them with his blood and bring each one home safely. Help them to make the right choices in all circumstances. Stay away from danger zones and familiarized safety areas in case they need to run.

Our Heavenly Father gracefully provides us with all the armor we need to stand against the wiles of the devil.

BELT OF TRUTH

As long as I knew my dad, he dressed before he came to the table to eat breakfast with the family. He would have on a white tee shirt tucked in his work pants and his belt was fastened around his waist. I don't know if he was raised that way as a child growing up in the Depression or if he got accustomed to that routine while serving in the US Army.

Never did I see him without a shirt and pants on around the house and not wearing a belt. The older I have become, I realize the belt was used to hold up his pants to prevent him from stumbling or falling down. And all that time, I thought he wanted to look like a gentlemen in front of his family. This was his dress routine till his death in 2005. Anyone who came to his funeral saw he had a shirt on with pants and around his waist was his very own Sunday's best belt.

In today's time, I notice there are not a lot of men who includes a belt with their everyday apparel. They put on a tee shirt along with pants and slip on flip flops. Then, they would open the door and they are gone with the wind. As you are watching them leave, you notice from looking from the back, their pants have slipped down to the middle of their buttocks.

Visualize that scene for a moment. How would they protect themselves if attacked if their pants are not in the proper place? People say that is the style now days. That style may get you seriously injured.

I am a mother that takes her children to school. I see a lot of young men wearing their shorts and even jeans down on the buttocks walking across a main street in town heading to school. The question is the same as the one mentioned before. How are they going to defend themselves and attack the assailant if approached for a dual?

As we grow in the Word, we attain a lot of territory (knowledge and truth). Similar, when we start off in grade school, then we move to middle school and high school. For some, after graduation, they will set out for a new frontier; College. After all that learning, they will take what they have learned and apply it towards a career.

As we grow and increase our knowledge of Christ, we get stronger and the devil does not like it one bit. The devil is the General of his army. He dispatches his soldiers to whomever he sees to inflict or oppress.

It is so important when we get attacked from the devil that we are fully equipped in God's Word. The more knowledgeable we are in his Word, the better. (ref: Luke 2:40) As we attain it, we as soldiers in the Lord's Army are to wrap it around our waist as a belt.

In Proverbs Chapter 3 verse 23 says, "Then shalt thou walk in the way safely, and thy foot shall not stumble." The belt holds your pants up; so, when you need to walk or run, you won't stumble and fall.

BREASTPLATE OF RIGHTEOUNESS

Most of us know that our heart is vital in keeping our body alive. Similar, in the way my son looks at peanut butter. He will eat a peanut butter sandwich three times a day if I let him. He will come home from school and go directly to the kitchen and open the icebox and take out the crackers; then, he will proceed to the storage cabinet and take out the peanut butter to put on those crackers.

After he had put on an inch of peanut butter on top of one cracker, he places another cracker on top of the peanut butter and the next blink it is gone. Just like that. Then, proceeds to fix another. To my son, peanut butter keeps him alive and well.

There is a lot of information out in this world how to stay fit and trim, eat better and what to do in a crises when the heart stops. Have you ever wondered why it is so important to protect our heart? Or, why should we guard it?

The heart has two primary goals. It receives and pumps blood. Sounds simple doesn't it. It has a 24/7 responsibility. Never rest. Never sleeps. Never takes a vacation.

The heart sends blood, provides our body with oxygen and nutrients and carries away waste. Out heart is one amazing muscle. The right side of the heart works with the left. Neither side is greater than the other.

Have you ever thought what the consequence would be if your heart don't allow the waste to exit? In the spiritual sense, it will slow down the anointing to flow in your life. In medical sense, a blockage will occur and eventually it will stop up the valves in your heart.

The Holy Spirit showed me that our heart receives the "Word" and the "Word" is then distributed thru out our body.

At any given time, if our blood stops flowing to any particular part of the body, the cells won't get oxygen that is distributed in the blood from our lungs, the cells will die. If the oxygen rich blood does not circulate as God intended, the person could die.

WASTE

Waste is defined as refuse (as garbage) that accumulates about habitations. Cities have designated days, either by contracting a waste treatment facility or by their own hired employees, when to come by and pick up residential and business garbage to be disposed. If you forget to take it to the street on the days the truck runs, you may find your waste stinking. And by the time the truck comes again within the week, the waste his piled up to the brim of the trash container carrying an outrageous odor that is out of this world.

Unfortunately, there are people who will not even take the time or effort to bring their trash to the street to be picked up. They just leave it around their house. When the odor gets to unbearable, then the neighbor calls the city's officials complaining about the smell of their neighborhood. The city's officials will come to investigate and give the offender so many days to clean up or risk being citied. They have a choice.

What is the waste in the heart of men? Have you ever thought about it? "Confession Time" I did not know till God showed me while studying the Breastplate of Righteousness.

One night at work, I was working on my work outcomes and my co-worker was really agitated with her life. Mr. Agitation tried his best to lure me into his web of confusion and I was not going in. I had to stop what I was doing and talk to her. I told her that I had something for her to read and I would bring it the next night. It is a poem I wrote year's prior how circumstances welcomed themselves into my life and by doing so, how God turned it for the Good.

The name of the poem, "The Day I Wore my Crown". I had received a Christmas card from a dear friend of the family and I placed it on my calendar in the dining room. One morning after exercise, I was sitting at the dining table and I glanced at the card while snacking on crackers before bed.

My attention was focusing on the caption of the card, "He Wore a Different Kind of Crown" I could not get that caption out of my mind. After receiving the card, the Lord gave me a dream. In the dream, he showed me a little girl kneeling beside her bed praying. As she was praying, I saw a hand reaching down and rested upon her head. She began to cry. As I looked closer, I saw her face expression changing. She looked like she was in a great deal of pain. The hand looked like the hand of an eagle. That eagle had its claws upon the child's head causing her a great deal of discomfort. She could not get away from his grip. The scene changed. He released his grip and as he did so, the hand changed back to the hand of the Father. After I saw the vision, I awoke.

As the week progressed, two people at work attacked me by using their attitude and I just could not figure out why. As I was going to my car after work, the Holy Spirit spoke to me and said, "You will not be able to overcome the big one till you master the little ones". I pondered those words while driving home. Shortly thereafter, I wrote my poem.

My biological mother had rejected me when I was born. The love between a mother and her newborn child did not exist. My sister and I were adopted into a family that loved kids and was willing to be parents to children that had no blood ties.

My biological mother knew who had adopted my sister and I and my adopted parents kept the door of communication opened in case she wanted to see us or come to visit. I was eight years old when she had another baby, a son.

For reasons unknown only to her, mom and dad was not offered to adopt him. She gave up her rights again as a mom and she let her youngest brother adopt him.

As time went by, rejection, bitterness and resentment made its residence in my heart. I had no idea how deep the wound was till the Holy Spirit opened my eyes. In the poem I wrote, "I cannot help to ask my Father, Was it me? Am I to blame? I stop and I listen and heard no sound—But in my heart he allowed me to see my crown. As I looked deeper within my heart—I could not help to notice it was identical to his while he was on the cross. It was strips of vine that were woven and braided—enter-locking together with thorns and briers. The thorns were causing him great pain and torment. And it appeared that the more he moved his head, it allowed the thorns to move deeper into his skin, causing the infected area to bleed.

It took some time to remove the thorn that was planted deeply into my mind by the enemy many years earlier. But there is nothing to big or great that God cannot do.

The thorn he removed was rejection. But there were many more vines with thorns and prickles. He will remove all the vines that cause my pain. He is Faithful and True. He will never mis-lead me or do me harm. He is the most gentle and kindest Father known to mankind. For all he wants is the best for you and me.

The thorn he was removing I thought was one. But oh! How I miscounted for there were more than just one. Bitterness and resentment are their names. These are my thorns that were causing all my pain.

When God's anointed hand ascended up, it allowed the thorns of this life to descend down and found rest upon my head. I could feel the pain and hurt that these two thorns caused. For I remember asking the Father distinctly, "Why Lord Why—What did I do wrong?"

And the Lord reminded me of the picture on my wall. That all of this time, I was actually wearing my Crown. A Crown he puts on me to test and try me. So, that in the end, I will be like him. An Over-Comer."

I told my co-worker that I felt that she has some, not a lot, resentment towards those who laid her off. She deigned what I told her. But it is true. She does not see it just yet. She will not be totally be healed till she confesses to the Lord and ask forgiveness and for his help.

Resentment and Bitterness has clasped themselves with her heart. Only God alone is able to break the bondage these two thorns have caused. As I continued working, the Holy Spirit showed me Resentment and Bitterness is "Waste". Waste that builds up over time till the "Word" overcomes it. Waste will block the anointing in your life. When "Truth" opens your eyes, open you heart unto him and let him pour out his love into you.

Love is never too strong or to weak
Love always considers some
one else's feelings
and not its own.
Love is always around to
pick you up when
feeling down and out.
Love is gentle and Love is kind.
Never goes where it is not welcome.
Always a gentlemen.
Love will always absolutely
overpower anything negative.
Love always does what it does best.
The capability to Love you back.
And never too far away from reach.

HELMET OF SALVATION

Have you ever been in a position or situation when the spirit of "Not Knowing" has the upper hand? I have. It does not matter what direction you turn to; until you conquer that spirit, the route is the same. Your days turn into nights and they are long. You don't know which way is up or down. All you know is that you exist.

You have advisors telling you what to do and the weight of despair has gotten a hold of your situation pulling you down into the depths of the unknown. As you are sinking, darkness overcomes you. You begin to wonder if Jesus knows where you are or even cares about you.

A few years ago a situation with "Now Knowing" came across my path at work. There was so much confusion and hurt among my co-workers that no one knew what to expect on a day-by-day basis. The president decided to lay off three thousand people. You could feel the tension in the air.

One night at work, I got some paper and wrote what was in my heart.

> God I am really scared.
> It is the "Not Knowing"
> that frightens me.
> I understand that you
> will hold my hand
> and whisper encouraging
> thoughts into my heart.
> Sayings that will up lift me
> and I hear don't worry,
> for I will always be by

your side—all the way.
You will smooth out my
doubts and calm
my fears—for you are
ALL-KNOWING.
I ask you a question.
Where is my peace?
Where is my joy?
Where is my happiness?
You provided all
three for me, But I let all
three slip thru my fingers.
I need all three back how
Can I cope without them I ask.
They are not in a drawer,
not in a closet,
most surely not under a bed.
They are right where I
Left them in the first place—
"In my heart"
Waiting for me for the asking.
Dear Father may I
have them back? I will keep
on asking you till
I get them back.
There you see that was not
too hard. All I
Did was Ask, Seek and
Knock.
Opened the door and
There they were—
Welcoming me back
With warming arms.

The poem gave me an opportunity to release my fear of termination. After I wrote this poem, I had a peace about the situation and I was able to just let it go and give it to the Lord.

Every year as long as I can remember my parents grew a garden. They would plant corn, peas, squash and tomatoes. They would try to plant anything they thought would take seed.

Dad loved fruit. He would plant figs, plums, pears and peaches. When harvest time came, mom would go and gather the fruit and start preserving.

You really don't need a lot equipment for preserving. Just the basics necessities: fruit, knife, cooking pot, sugar, sure jell, jars and your time.

When the cooking was over, she would set out filling the jars up with the fruit; then, she would let the fruit cool down before putting her accomplishment in the cabinet for later use.

As long as the jars lids are tight and the glass does not crack, the fruit will remain fresh and enjoyable. Even though the fruit in the jar is cooked and ready to eat after sealing, its taste and looks are better in the days ahead. Why? Time. Time has a way to clean out the debris and begin a fresh new look.

I remember looking at mom's preserved pears after sitting in jars after 24 hours. They looked clearer and clean. The color of the fruit had time to gather its natural beauty that God intended.

Let me ask you a question. How is the fruit that lives within you? Have you taken a look lately? Is it safe to share it among others? If you discover that your fruit is not fresh and preservation is dying, all you need to do is ask Jesus to come and take out the debris and refill your heart with his love. And, he will come in and restore you fully.

Occasionally, I will have something different for supper. My family loves pizza. After I place the order, the pizza usually arrives within 45-50 minutes. Before I can receive my order, I pay the ticket and the delivery person opens up the case that keeps the food warm and reaches in and pull out my order and I reach out and receive.

The point I want to make is that is how Christ comes to us. He is invited because we asked him to come by. He has something we need and he wants to give it to us.

He reaches in his heart and forgives us for all of our past wrong doings and we reach out and receive his forgiveness. And his forgiveness is already paid for. I don't have to scramble for change because the debt was paid in full on the Cross at Calvary.

In the book of John, chapter 10 verse 10, the Word says, "The thief does not come except to steal, and to kill and to destroy". NJKV

Are you aware when the fire department receives a call during the night, their clothing is laid out in an orderly fashion at the end of their bed? Hats, gloves and jackets have a proper place in route to the truck to keep down frustration, confusion and panic when the alarm goes off.

The experienced fire fighters give advice to others to always be thinking, stop and take a deep breath and get into healthy habits that will help them on their calls. Doing these tactics will help prepare them for the task at hand.

When the call comes, their mind is driving faster than they can imagine. They train themselves from the physical prospective down to their intellectual and emotional reactions. Having the right frame of mind can mean all the difference in the world.

We never know what lies ahead of us while we journey thru this world. Being prepared from all sides is a must. We need to keep ourselves fully trained and ready so that when we do meet our opponent, "Not Knowing", we will be able to face him with the knowledge that God has placed within us and conquer him for good.

We never know when the Lord will use us to full fill his will. When that times does come, he has already preserved us for the task and we will go willingly wearing our Helmet of Salvation.

SHIELD OF FAITH

The Romans shield was four feet long and two in a half feet wide. It mostly protected them better. As history informs us, they learned the advantage of the longer and wider shield's protection.

As a convoy, the Romans would fit their rectangular shields together to form a well-defined roof and wall to their front sides protecting them from flying arrows and burning fat that flew above them.

The main goal was to press forward and kill as many men while pursuing to get on the other side. As the soldier pursued forward, he would hold his shield in front of himself so that the force of the impact would knock down the enemy to the ground.

The Romans put a lot of faith into their war equipment, not in God. They, like us, discovered that equipment does fail and as time presses forward, equipment advances to higher levels.

We have so much confidence in our inventors and supply companies to keep us a float that we, like the Romans, have forgotten who really equips us the knowledge in the first place.

When I cannot pay my electric bill on time, I don't put my Faith into the power company to help me out. I put my Faith in God's Word where he said he would supply my needs.

My Faith in God's Word is my shield of protection. How? By learning his Word and taking that knowledge to use as a defense to work for me not against me.

The more I learn of God, the more knowledge I attain and when the Devil comes against me, I use the "Word" to fight him.

In the middle of the Romans shield facing the enemy is a weapon called the "Boss". It is used to attack and knock down the offender. The Boss represents to us the "Word" and the shield represents the Knowledge in God's Word.

It is noted their shield was made out of compressed plywood and held together by glue. Had a resistance to cracking, shrinkage, twisting, warping and recognized by its high degree of strength. Among those listed, it was also strong and flexible.

The Shield not only protects you; also, used as an instrument to drive you through your battles. The more we press on and conquer, the more we believe in his Word and attain Faith in him.

Learning is a process and as we attain that knowledge, the more we are aware of God's presence in our lives.

SCANDALS OF PEACE

Several years ago, I joined a fitness center in Texas City, Texas. The participation of this gym is awesome. All ages can come and socialize with their own peers and work out at the same time. Some time while back, one of the elders came to me and asked me if I ran. I told him no. Running and I are not the best of friends. He encouraged me to go outside with him and let him be the judge if I could run or not. I ended up running all around the city's square. I felt good about myself and I wanted to keep on running.

He told me the first thing I need to do was get the proper shoes. At the time, the nearest sporting store was in League City, twenty-five miles north of town. When I located the section for the shoes, I did not know which brand to choose; so, I tried on shoes till I got the right one for my feet.

Not everybody is created the same. There are those who have a high arch and needs extra support. Some are flat footed. They need a certain shoe to give them support and cushion in areas of the feet while running.

I remember needing another pair of shoes and I went to another sporting store in Webster, Texas. Again, I tried several pairs of different shoes. When I found the brand I liked, the store's clerk told me to go outside and run up and down the sidewalk to get the feel of the shoe. Any discomfort to either foot, that brand may not provide enough support and cushion to meet the need to run safely.

When I got home, I took the shoes out of the box and prepared them for the next day for a three-mile run. I started a new relationship between my feet and the new member of the family, Saucony.

Saucony worked well with my feet. I was tired after the three mile run; my feet however, handled the pressure real well. Anything we do, we have to prepare ourselves for whatever the task requires including the equipment.

Our mind and body may be ready; however, if we don't have all the necessities, we are wasting our time and energy and setting ourselves up for failure.

My nephew, James, had a softball game during mother's day weekend. I wanted to go to watch him play for I have not seen him play all season. So, my mom and I went to the ballpark to watch him play ball. As I watched, I noticed their shoes, there were cleats to help stabilize their balance as they attempt to hit the ball. The more they practiced with their shoes, the body and their mind will interact as a whole to work together and win the battle.

I have accomplished several marathons, 5k's and some 10k's in the past twelve years. Thru out these races, I have kept up with my equipment (feet) that God has gracefully given to me to fulfill not only my desire but also his will for my life.

Whatever your task for the day may be; whether it is shopping, playing ball or yard work, be prepared at all times. ". . . because your adversary the devil, as a roaring lion, walketh about, seeking whom he may devour; Whom resist steadfast in the faith, knowing that the same afflictions are accomplished in your brethren that are in the world". I Peter 5:8 and 9.

Those children on the softball team have learned to stand firm by pressing their shoes within the soil so that the cleats on the bottom of their shoes can give them the stability they need to hold their ground to hit the ball.

Likewise, we should do when the enemy comes to attack us. We are to stand firm in our foundation, God's Word and resist the Devil.

SWORD of the SPIRIT

As a child growing up, my dad has several knives. He would occasionally place one onto a steel block and sharpen the knife while watching TV. I hardly saw him use his knife; but when I did, I can recall the sharpness it had.

Tools and knives go back for several centuries. The biggest improvement in the 1st century A.D. was the introduction to the double edge blades. According to history, the double edge blades really made a big impact during the roman world in the Republican Period.

The double edge blade went thru six steps before it was ready to be used as a sword. The first stage is to purify the ore by removing the physical dirt using water. The water washed away physical impurities on the surface.

Then, they took the ore to the iron mill where the ore was crushed into pieces. Charcoal was laid down with the crushed ore on top. As the charcoal burned, the water was driven out of the ore; however, oxygen was still present. To get rid of the oxygen, they placed the ore into a small furnace called a bloomer. The bloomer was sealed to keep oxygen in the air getting into the mix.

Fire needs oxygen to burn; therefore, the oxygen is pulled out of the ore. Other impurities melt and flow out in the form of slag. Good iron is collected in a soft mass in the bottom of the bloomer and this is the beginning of sword blades.

They took the bloom to their town's blacksmith where it was heated in his hearth and hammered into a workable condition which was important because this was the final step to get rid of the last impurities.

The blacksmith takes the metal and places it on the anvil. Using the hammer, he would pound the metal into a blade while using his tongs. As the metal cooled, he would reheat it to keep it workable. The blacksmith repeatedly reheats the iron and hammers away. When the blade meets the blacksmith's specification, it is ready to be quenched.

Quenching gives the blade strength and the metal becomes hard. The downside of quenching makes the blade brittle; therefore, it goes thru one more stage called tempering.

The metal is reheated a final time to a specific temperature. The temperature is raised to determine the blade's hardness and how it will keep its edge.

As you can see, the preparation of the sword takes time, planning and skillful eyes to achieve its quality and successfulness to be a double edge sword.

Even thru all its stages of development, the one holding the sword has just as many stages of preparation to be ready at any given time to fight.

As the soldier prepares himself as a warrior, the Holy Spirit prepares us when we go against the Devil.

My dad did his part teaching all three of us, Sissy, Michael and me, the importance of learning God's Word. He started us by learning the scripture by memory and graduating too quoting the memory verse in front of the body of Christ, the church.

A verse in Psalms 23 says, "I will fear no evil for thou are with me". As we learn his Word, we attain knowledge and faith, our eyes focuses on truth, our ear hears his voice, our mouth speaks Life into our very being and our body receives restoration.

The Holy Spirit gives the Word its penetrative ability and sharp edge. Having the Holy Spirit residing with us, he equips, teaches and shields us from the devil's evilness.

When the devil approaches us to do evil, we have the power to send him away with the Word of God.

CHAPTER SEVEN

SEVERAL YEARS AGO a friend of mine told me there is a gem living inside every person. I did not fully understand at that time what he meant till I started studying the creation of gems.

It is amazing to me how God takes certain ingredients from the soil, round up abundance of heat and pressure, a phrase of cooling, time and space to build to receive the beautiful results found in gems.

One may not put this gem in the spotlight to represent growth; however, I find all the concepts of growth well with the perimeter of the creation of this beautiful gem. For, this gem can take you on a voyage you will not forget.

It has been said that growing up is hard to do. I can relate. Adulthood can be overwhelming at times. There have been times where I want to turn back the clock when I was nine years old.

The only responsibility I had was to make sure the animals were fed when I got home from school and the eggs gathered and placed in containers in the ice box. A simple and not too hard responsibility; unfortunately, time must prevail.

Chrysolite (Periodot) is birth on rocks floating in the earth's mantle 20 to 55 miles below the surface. They are brought up near the surface by activity of pressure involving activity and movement of continental plates.

As time presses forward, weathering and erosion brings them to the surface. Being at the right place at the right time, people who love to adventure out of their comfort zone and too explore may come across these gems while hiking up a mountain or bike riding mountainous terrain.

Growth of the Periodot is not easy during its transformation. Some will survive while others may perish. Passages or space are constantly opening and closing. When space becomes available for growth, pressure and temperature are at its highest.

When growth stops and restarts again this will allow new layers to birth; however, these new layers will not always bond completely among it peers and this is one of the reasons for inclusions within a stone.

Our growth as a child of God and the Periodot has some interesting seminaries in this vastness cycle we call life; even though, worlds apart.

Sometimes, we get off the road that God has destined us to be on just to live it up to see if we can do it without God. "I want to do it my way" sort of thing.

Some have discovered that road of life is not all what it is up to be and turned around and headed back into the direction that God had intended for them. Unfortunately some don't return.

While you were on your own, you experienced the well with the bad, overcame obstacles, met new friends and found yourself surrounded by an overwhelming sense of loneliness.

Life of the past won't bond with your new life with Christ. (2 Corinthians 5:17) Remember those inclusions within the stone? It is been noted that this gem is uncomplicated but not for the cutter. The crystals are rough, cunning and very easy to break. There is a great deal of tension inside each crystal.

You may not go back to the way you once lived; however, the choices you made while living there will always be a constant reminder of your past.

Our Father is aware of the struggles we have to face every day. He knows the "end time" is upon us and the pressure is enormous. This is one of the reasons why he sent his only begotten Son to go thru those pressure points and overcome them so when we have to face them, we are not alone; for, he has embed into us the endurance to fight and be an overcomer.

A skillful hand is vital to bring out the beauty of this stone. Once the cutter has succeeded in removing the coarser inclusions, its glory is greatly admired.

CHAPTER EIGHT

THE BERYL GEM is created by the Hydrothermal Process. This process involves water. As rain comes down from heaven and nourishes the earth, some of the water will find cracks in the soil and lodge there where it will be heated by the upwelling's of the magma from the mantle and become a hydrothermal solution.

Most of the time this solution is driven by convection. Convection is a circulatory motion in a fluid due to warmer portion rising and cooler density portions sinking. In other words, hot water rises and cool water sinks.

These movements occur through cracks and channels in the rock forcing the water to move slowly; and while it is moving, it stays in constant contact with other minerals.

What is so interesting about water convection through rock? It is an effective means of dissolving, transporting and depositing minerals.

As I was studying this gem and on the hydrothermal process, the Holy Spirit brought to my attention to Moses asking God to let him see his glory and what he will do for us while living under the shadows of the Almighty.

We can find this story in the book of Exodus, Chapter 33. Moses went in the tabernacle to meet with God. As he was there, he asked God to show him his glory.

"And he said, Thou canst not see my face: for there shall no man see me and live. And the Lord said Behold, there is a place by me, an thou shalt stand upon a rock: and it shall come to pass, while my glory passeth by that I will put thee in a cleft of the rock, and will cover thee with my hand while I pass by: And I will take away mine hand and thou shalt see my back parts: but my face shall not be seen."

Years ago, I heard a song title, "He is still working on me." The more I study on this particular gem, the Holy Spirit has shown me the effectiveness of this extraordinary beautiful gem.

Dissolve means to loosen; to destroy; to bring to an end. I find it fascinating the first stage of this gem is the first stage of a "New Believer" in Christ. When we ask Christ to be Lord over our life and invite him into our heart, something wonderful happens. He starts working on us to be like him. He enters our heart and we begin a new chapter.

Most people know that without blood we cannot live. The blood runs thru our veins to bring nourishment to keep us alive. As a new believer, the Word of God travels in our veins to bring us healing, nourishment, attacks evil, sends conviction and forgiveness.

The Word gets behind doors and breaks the chains where we have stored up hardness and bitterness and breaks it and loosens it to where conviction can enter our heart.

As it dissolves issues of the flesh, it is making room to transport fulfillment. For some people, it has been a long time since they felt good about themselves. They look and feel great. Their long and sad face becomes alive and vibrant as the Holy Spirit manifest himself thru them.

They have a song in their heart as they perform their duties. They look forward to every new day. The wind may blow, mountains may rise and water may cease; but, it will not stop them for the glory of the Lord is their strength.

As the Word changes and prepares us, the world is watching. He has placed you where you are right now to be an instrument for him.

I was a student for a short while at Southwestern Bible College near Dallas Texas in the early 80's. I did not associate very much with the other students; however, they sure did notice me.

As the fall quarter began to close, if you were not returning, you had to clean up your room in order to get your room deposit back. As I began to look for boxes, one of the dorm's occupants came to help me. When we located the boxes, we turned around and headed back to my room.

On the way back, she began to thank me for teaching her the importance of a successful studier. She had rather socialize than prioritize and her grade performance lacked.

She noticed I did not go places. I stayed in my room and studied. You never know who is watching you. God has placed you where you are needed and in turn to be a blessing to others.

As you fulfill your destiny, be a blessing to others. Leave them something to remember you by. Leave a legacy, even if all you have to offer is your smile.

CHAPTER NINE

YEARS AGO, I studied King David's accomplishments. On one occasion before he was appointed King, there was a Philistine in the region named Goliath. His height was over 9 feet and he knew that the children of Israel were afraid of him due to his height and statue. Israel could not achieve victory over the Philistines because of their champion, Goliath.

One day, David took parched corn and bread to his brothers who were at the battle field fighting against the Philistines. He heard Goliath speaking against the children of God and it angered him. He went thru out the camp and inquired what would happen to the man who conquerors Goliath.

King Saul heard about David inquiring about the situation at hand and had him sent unto him. David told Saul that he would confront Goliath. Saul was concerned about him approaching him because of his youthfulness and that Goliath was classified as a "Man of War".

David insured Saul that he was able to conquer Goliath. Goliath saw David and scorned him due to his youthfulness and his fair appearance and cursed David by his gods. David told Goliath the God of Israel will deliver him into his hands.

I want you to notice what happens next. Goliath roused up and came to meet David. David hastened and ran towards Goliath with his sling in his hand. He reached into his bag and pulled out one stone. David laid that stone in the sling and he began to twirl his sling above his head into the wind. When David heard that familiar pitch sound, he released the sling and the stone was guided by the Holy Spirit and lodged into Goliath's forehead. There he fell upon his face in front of David.

There is so much opposition in the world today to where it is so easy to lose focus. When opposition surfaces, instead of running for cover, face it head on. David did not run from his conflict. Instead, he faced his opponent and stayed focused while the feelings of pressure surrounded him.

David did not allow his anger towards Goliath to overpower him. As David looked him in the face and spoke to him directly, David did not move towards the left or to the right but stood firmly in one place and faced Israel's Fear and by the direction of the Holy Spirit, Israel triumphantly won a mighty battle against Fear and being controlled emotionally.

This story about conquering our giants is all about the making of the stone Topaz. Hot magma rises from the earth's mantle but fails to erupt as a volcano. The cooled magma forms granite veins in the earth's crust. Here imbedded in these veins is where Topaz crystals are formed.

As I studied this stone it carries the attribute how to manage your emotions. Believe me; I can use a lot of guidance in this territory.

When you are confronting your giant, here are some guidelines that all of us need to be aware of.

(1) Quit allowing anger to take over
(2) Stay centered in pressure situations
(3) Stop avoiding conflict (lean into the conflicts and resolve them so you can re-organize your life to include New Learning)
(4) Stop getting so worked up over little things
(5) Keep mistakes from throwing you into a tailspin
It is so important to deal with problems correctly and promptly
(6) Choose how you would respond to difficult situations and people
(7) Keep anger from damaging relationships
Use anger constructively
(8) Maintain emotional clarity in the midst of change
(9) Eliminate behaviors and habits that work against you

God has graciously given us the ability to overcome all of life's difficulties as conquerors thru his son, Jesus. Every triumph we overcome in this life has its own special stone as a remembrance of all its making of a victorious overcomer.

CHAPTER TEN

I REMEMBER THE night when I told my husband we are going be parents. His response was "Oh no! Not us". Time swiftly passed forward and Dalton was born and in the eyes of new parents, he was perfect. By the grace of God, is now 19 years old, graduated from TCHS and in his first year of college.

Achievements and advancements along with life's ups and downs, pulling us in all directions and equipping us for a life of success along with disappointments is what growth is all about.

God created all things; and while in the process of creating, there is "Time" for growth. For some, growth will excel beyond the boundaries of what we call "Normal"; while on the other hand, growth will stay on the beaten path that is was designed to be on.

I am not talking about how tall or short we are. It is taking one plus another to equal a solution. Memorize the outcome and later down the road, you will reap the knowledge you have obtained.

Growth is the reason why people have assets. We as humans, in this day in time, have to protect what is ours; if not, we will lose everything that we have worked for. Therefore, we need to protect all our investments.

In the book of Matthew Chapter 10 verse 10, the Word says the enemy comes to steal, kill and destroy. He does not care which adverb (how, why and when) he uses just as long he gets his job accomplished.

In this century, people have invested a lot of money, time and effort to protect their home and property from intruders. If you are one of those that have invested in an alarm system for your home, did you take thought into investing a protection system for the house that secures your heart?

Think about that for a moment. Our heart absorbs a lot of emotional stress as well as experiencing just the normal outcomes of daily activity.

We live in a hustle and bustle society. A lot of us don't realize just how much we put into a 24 hour period. People are always on the go; even after retirement, they travel great distances to see grandkids and do other things they wanted to do earlier in life but their jobs need their undivided attention.

They get wrapped up into the moment and forget about the stress their body is absorbing. I have had people to tell me they get used to it. That may be true; however, all it is doing is putting stress on their body and one day, they will reap the outcome.

Why don't you let me encourage you to take a moment and write down what you do every night of the week. As you review your list, if you are out and about more than recouping from your days of labor, you are heading for disaster in health sense. Slow down and enjoy life while you are still able.

This may sound familiar to some of you out there. Indulge me for a moment. Visualize yourself on the days that you have ball practice after work and you rush home to pick up the kids to be on time at the ballpark. There was no time to stop and eat. Now you are in the stands watching your kids play ball and your stomach is groaning for it is hungry. There is a concession stand near the entrance. You make a way down the steps to grab a hotdog on a bun. The more you get closer to the concession stand your stomach says, "Feed me".

You load up the hotdog to the brim. You say to yourself, "I will probably pay for his later on tonight". The meat was most likely loaded with a lot of sodium and preservatives that are not healthy for your heart. We all need to watch what we put into our body; however, there are more entrances we need to observe. Can you guess what they are?

FIVE ENTRANES

When I growing up, my dad was the director over the Children Church department. He loved to hear the kids sing. One of the songs he taught them was "Oh Be Careful".

In the song, the words remind our children to be careful what they see, hear, speak and touch and the road they take in life. He used that song to teach them the influences of the world would have on them as they grow to maturity and then after.

Let's talk about sight for a moment. Babies, when they reach eight months old, they can begin to recognize people and objects that are close to them. Do you recall what the number 8 means? Let me refresh your memory. "New Beginning"

At the end of the eight-month period, their world takes on a new perspective. Their eyes have learned to focus and track movement, distinguish differences which in time become clearer and begin to see the small things of life.

Perception means how you look at things. Your perception makes the difference of your meaning and action as the method you perceive. As we get older, our perception changes as we encounter the different stages of life. As we graduate to a higher level, so does our perception because our knowledge has increased.

Let me ask you another question. Once you obtained the knowledge, how did you put it to work?

How do we know if it is ok to look upon something if you don't know it is wrong? My perception of what is right or wrong may well be different than my husband's. Why? Different parents who believe differently raise us.

New parents raise their children by two sets of guidelines. The basic fundamental of no no's is the first to be introduced. Then, the challenge gets tougher as the child grows older due to each parent upbringing.

There have been times when my husband and I do not see eye to eye especially on certain circumstances when asked if it is right or wrong for our children to take a part in. The decision is divided. There have been times we have agreed.

As their mom, I have to ask the question to myself is it safe, educational, profiting or worth the money for my children to take part. There are a lot of areas in this life that is not safe for our children. The cost could be great. Are you willing to be a part of that cost?

I have raised my children the way I believe that will offer them success; however, at any given time, one or both of them can rebel and refuse to walk the path that I have shown them and they may find themselves into a lot of trouble.

As parents, we should not let our children leave the homestead without the necessary essentials. Those essentials are vital for their protection, guidance to keep them in focus and provide awareness strategies if or when tragedy strikes.

EAR

My husband, Adam, loves to fish. We would on occasionally go to the Texas City Dike and spend most of the day fishing and have some fun. As he got older, his desire to fish grew and he decided to purchases a boat to take him further into the Gulf to catch bigger fish.

I recall one weekend he invited a friend of ours to go fishing. We anchored behind Stewart Beach on the east side of Galveston Texas. The current that day was rough. The boat would not be still and I ended up laying down on the bow because I could stand up. Ended up, Brian was the only one standing and catching fish; therefore, we did not stay there long.

We decided to anchor up and head toward the Jetty where the water is a lot calmer. It was not long after we found a spot to fish, Adam and I were enjoying our fellowship with our friend Brian.

Balance is one of the keys how we get things accomplished. Without it, we would not be successful in anything we do.

Balancing our lives is like balancing our bank account. If there is not enough funds in your account, you must refrain yourself from spending. Unfortunately, there are some that will overdraft themselves paying a fee for every return check.

Meaning, we all need to be careful and watch every step we take in our life. For one minute, we are on track, everything is in order and moving along like it should; and then the next minute, our world is crashing down all around us.

Unfortunately, not everyone is raised by parents who care for their children's well-being. For those who do, they provide guidelines or advice; especially, when their children are surrounded by the "unknown".

Those guidelines are crafted to keep them in focused and balanced so when they are approached they won't sway between the left and right hand which causes them to get dizzy and lose their insight.

Not all circumstances require a physical resolution to get back on track. Sometimes a spoken Word and an ear to receive is all it takes.

Our mouth will either bring
refreshing revival or a visit to the pit;
A gate for our emotions to be revealed;
A gateway to teach and to release your knowledge;
A gateway for praise and worship;
A gateway to release uncertainty;
A gateway to express love and thankfulness;
A gate to receive forgiveness and too
Be forgiven
And
A way to Freedom

HAND

We need to be watchful what we take into our custody. Our hands are the principal organ of touch, an active member of the body and chief employed in active duty.

What happens when we go shopping for Christmas gifts? We pick out our favorite places to shop where we can get good deals for our money. We look around and check out the new arrivals and prices.

When we see something that we think that mom or dad would like, we go and investigate. We take it off the shelf and bring it closer to our eyes and we examine it. Then, we look to see how much it cost.

If it is a candle, we again bring it closer to our eyes and then we smell it. Speaking of myself, there are times while I shop, I wonder if they will like it; and before I know it, I am asking myself out loud that question and then turn around and answer myself back. Don't you be bashful. You know you do it too.

As we handle the item in our hand, we come to a conclusion in our mind if we want to purchase it or not. We either welcome the item into our custody or place it back on the shelf leaving it there for its next inspection. I don't believe that some of us realize just how much passes thru our hands on a day-by-day basis.

Our hands come in contact with all sorts of metal, plastics, paper goods, glass and food necessities just to name a few. Whatever we do touch, we don't know what or who has touched it before our hands handled it.

As these items progress into their purpose, they contain knowledge, elements of our earth, sweat from hours of creation, time and desire. These are just a fraction of the ingredients that are involved in creating something useful and beautiful.

On the road of progressing, it is unfortunate to inform you these items may pick up unwanted guest. These guests may infect your body in a way that you may not imagine.

It is so vital to keep abreast at all times. Stay alert and watch where you allow your hands to touch. Instead of being used or drawn to destruction, allow your hands to guide you and others to "Victory".

FEET

In order for us to move forward and grow, the Lord has provided mountains for us to climb and valleys to cross. As we attempt the summit and walk thru the valleys, there awaits great achievements for us to accomplish.

One thing I have learned as a runner, I have to make sure my feet are taken care of. One way to succeed is to make sure I wear the proper shoes for the right race. If I don't, I will be in trouble.

Regardless if the race is on pavement or trail, shoes and feet need to be in top shape condition. To sum it all up, to master the mountain, buy the proper shoes and prepare your feet for a journey of a life time. If you are up for the challenge, it will be tough; but, worth the reward afterwards.

The roads at some of the races are not in all good shape condition. I have to be in a constant awareness mode. Cracks, rocks, even pot holes are common and one slip; I can twist my ankle and be out of the race.

As I mentioned previously, it is vital that we stay alert. We can sway towards the right or left and before we realize, we have gotten off our road of deliverance.

The devil can use just about anything to distract you. We need to keep our eyes on the prize and in the end we will be victorious.

Years ago, the small community of Athens, Texas decided to have a 5k and 10k run. I decided that I wanted to run in this race; so, we packed up and headed for my parents' house in Palestine.

Next day, Adam and I left early for the 45 minute trip and rain was pouring down. The rain had stopped just in time before the race began. The runners gathered to the starting line. The gun sounded and we took off.

It started off great. I passed up people and some passed me. I had never ran in this race; so, as I was running, I observed my surroundings. Athens is a beautiful city.

I heard one of the participants mentioning the turnaround for the 5k was behind us where two guys were standing giving people water. I had missed the turnaround. I turned around and headed back in the opposite direction to finish the race.

It can be so easy to get distracted these days; especially, when there is a lot of drama taking place around you. Stay alert and prepare yourself at all cost. For, your reward will be waiting for you in the end.

CHAPTER ELEVEN

MY IMAGINATION CAN only speculate what our earth looked like when God created, by his Word, the world into existence.

As God allowed seasons too come and go, the world proceeded to change. With that change, there were "New Beginnings and Endings". As each season ended, they would leave behind treasures that would be discovered for centuries to come. One of those treasures would be the Jacinth stone.

For centuries, chemist studied Jacinth and came to find out in order to bring out the beauty of this stone you need three things. Lots of heat, a furnace and Zirconium. To show you how these three work in unity, I need for you to indulge me, a little, to tell you in a story form.

In the early part 2000, my co-worker, and friend told me she was retiring in January after her birthday. Not long after retirement, she moved away from the coast and moved back to her home town in Louisiana.

Her relationship with Jesus was so solid not even a jack hammer with an axe end could penetrate thru her relationship with Christ. As time proceeded forward, she continued to live her life to the fullest. She continued to attend church every Sunday morning including Wednesday's prayer meetings. As her relationship grew with the church, she made new friends and welcomed them into her home to have weekly fellowship time.

She got caught up with making friends and fellowshipping with them that she forgot her "First Love". One by one her friends stopped coming by. She would leave them messages and when they called her back, she would ask them if she had offended them in anyway. Their reply was always no. As more of her friends separated themselves from her, the more her heart broke.

I have known of her as a spiritual leader and a prayer warrior. She and I would study the Word at work. She would pick out a scripture to study and we would bring out our Bibles and we would take apart every word and study it by using our concordance.

As she as going thru this transition she noticed that her prayer and fellowship time with the Lord had been pushed back. When she did pray for people, the anointing she once knew was nowhere to be found. It was like praying to a wall. She wanted to know why; so, she asked the Holy Spirit why? He showed her that she had distanced herself from him and he wanted her back.

The desire of wanting her "First Love" returned. She gave up TV and fellowship with family to get back what she had allowed to slip away from her. She told me she was backsliding and did not realize it. It happened very slowly, cautiously, and not suddenly.

She was experiencing being complacence in her relationship with Christ.

As she was telling me this, I was remembering another friend that was very close to the Lord and the same thing happened to her. Her family began to have trails involving their son's life style and before the church realized it, they had completely stopped attending. The spiritual people in the church began to pray for them and the Holy Spirit showed one of the prayer warriors a ship on a voyage. The captain had his route planned; but, the driver behind the wheel got his mind off the captain's route and the ship begin to drift off course.

It is so easy to allow the world to influence us in areas of our daily walk that we don't realize until it is upon us that by inviting the world into our lives that it will try to take preference over the course that God has laid out for us.

This happens to all of us at one time of another. Thank the Lord for the Holy Spirit that when we do drift off course, he uses reinforcements to bring us back. When we are gone from his presence, there has to be a cleansing thereafter. We did not attain the influences of the world in one day. It was done slowly. The Holy Spirit has to cleanse as the same way.

We ask for forgiveness and Christ's forgives; however, the attachments of the world are still there and must be removed. God puts us into his furnace and turns up the heat to break apart what the world has attached in us.

The less of the world's influences, the more of his son he sees and the world sees Jesus. As we go thru the trails of this life, dealing with the pressure and heat that surrounds us, we are able to withstand the fire; for, the Holy Spirit blankets us with the "Word". And as the world watches, they are watching a miracle in the process. Instead of the fire and pressure destroying us, the "Word" takes the fire and uses it as a reflection of him and as the world watches you, they see Jesus in the fire and we are not harmed.

CHAPTER TWELVE

DON'T WE ALL love to read a book or article that starts with an interesting beginning, the middle keeps our curiosity flowing and the ending captures our heart?

The life of the Amethyst stone so happens to portray the same theme. It starts as molten lava that cools down and sets over a period of time. When an air bubble appears and more volcanic rock tops the air bubble, an Geode is formed.

All of this activity happens when the bubble is hot. As the heavens brings refreshment upon the earth with rain, chemicals, trapped inside the rock will be able to be released into the water. The water gets absorbed and passes thru the hard rocky outside layer of the rock and gets trapped within the bubble.

As time presses forward, crystals are formed as water is constantly moving and depositing more minerals to the inside of the hollow air bubble.

When iron impurities are found inside the Geode, the crystals have a purple/violet color. This purple/violet color becomes more intense in the tips of the crystals.

As I was pondering on all the stages of the Amethyst being birth, the Holy Spirit bought to mind a familiar story. It is a story that will move you. By the time the end draws near, your heart is captured by an "Amazing Grace".

As my sister and I were growing up in the sixties, our mom made the majority of our clothes. When the nineties strove around, it was cheaper to buy or clothes and a lot of stores just did not carry the amount of material as year's prior.

Mother made sure her dresses looked magnificent including the hem. Before she hemmed the garment, we had to put it on and turn around a few times so she could see if the pins held the edge of the garment straight. Then, she would hem the piece either by hand or machine.

After completion, we put it on for a last time for her to look it over and to be sure she had done a good job. As always, her work was great. She spent a lot of time making sure that all her effort was successful.

As the Lord reminded me in all clothes whether it is a shirt, jacket, end of a sleeve or pants, there is a hem. The purpose of the hem is to prevent snagging, tearing and separation. (Represents the Word of God)

In the book of Matthew 9:20-22, there is lady that had been sick for twelve years. She went thru many physicians to find what the cause of her dilemma and the cure of her aliment and doing so, she spent all of her savings. None of the doctors was able to meet her need and since she had this problem, she was considered as a outcast and was not permitted around people.

She had heard of Jesus healing the blind and all sorts of illnesses'. Wanting to be normal, healed and not an outcast, became her deepest desire to where she did not care of customs, rules and regulations of the day.

As the day approached for Jesus to appear on the shore of Galilee, she was there waiting for the right moment to reach out and take hold what she had heard about his special anointing to heal.

She wanted to be free. She could taste it. Desired it. She did not want to settle for a little taste of his healing power. She desired a full amount.

Out of pure desperation and nothing to lose, she pressed forward and fell down and took hold of his presence (hem) and held it tightly and when she felt his anointing power being released within her, she knew without a doubt she had been made whole.

She unleashed her faith in the "Word" and stayed behind as Christ was pushed forward by the crowd. Knowing that his miraculous power had been released, asked "Who touch me"? He looked around and being "All Knowing" saw her in his mist and told her that her faith had made her whole.

Her example of faith should be a great inspiration too us all. Reminding us not to settle for a taste but to take hold and receive a full amount.